This Walker Book belongs to:

_____

_____

Charles Dickens'
Oliver Twist

For Iggy, with love

First published 2002 in *Charles Dickens and Friends*
by Walker Books Ltd, 87 Vauxhall Walk, London SE11 5HJ

This edition published 2014

1 3 5 7 9 10 8 6 4 2

© Marcia Williams 2014, 2007, 2002

The right of Marcia Williams to be identified as author/illustrator of this work
has been asserted by her in accordance with the Copyright, Designs and Patents Act 1988

This book has been typeset in Kennerly Regular

Printed and bound in Great Britain by Clays Ltd, St Ives plc

British Library Cataloguing in Publication Data:
a catalogue record for this book is available from the British Library

ISBN 978-1-4063-5692-2

Charles Dickens'

Oliver Twist

Retold and Illustrated by

Marcia Williams

WALKER BOOKS
AND SUBSIDIARIES
LONDON · BOSTON · SYDNEY · AUCKLAND

Contents

Chapter One
Treats of Oliver Twist's Birth and Board

Among the buildings in English Victorian towns there often stood a house for the poor, known as the workhouse. On the night this story begins, a young girl collapsed in the street and was carried into one. Her shoes were worn with walking and she was heavily pregnant. Where she came from, or where she was going to, nobody knew.

The next day, in the presence of a parish doctor and a drunken nurse, she gave birth to a baby boy named Oliver. For some time, he lay poised between life and death. Then, after a few struggles, he breathed, sneezed and let out a cry. As Oliver gave this first proof that he was alive, his pale-faced mother raised herself feebly from her pillow and whispered, "Let me see the child, and die."

Oliver's poor mother hardly had the

strength to hold him in her arms. She kissed Oliver once with her sweet, pale lips, closed her eyes and died.

Her family could not be traced, nor could Oliver's father. As Oliver lay wrapped in a blanket, it was impossible to tell if he was the child of an aristocrat or of a beggar. But now, as the drunken nurse dressed him in an old calico cloth, which had grown yellow with use, it was quite clear that he was nothing more than a workhouse orphan. Like all the other half-starved orphans, he would be despised by all and pitied by none. Oliver began to cry lustily. If he could have known that he was now an orphan, perhaps he would have cried even louder!

Oliver was given the surname "Twist"

by Mr Bumble, the parish beadle, and left in the care of an elderly woman. She was a cruel old lady and she fed the babies in her care on the smallest possible amount of weak gruel, leaving them rolling about on the floor. Those that did not die from starvation often sickened and died of neglect or even fell into the fire, but Oliver had a sturdy spirit and somehow he survived these years of neglect.

By the age of nine, Oliver looked younger than his years. He was short in stature and very pale and thin. However, Mr Bumble thought him ready to learn a trade and join the other workhouse children. These poor, ragged youngsters were fed on three meals of watery gruel a day, an onion twice a

week and half a roll on Sundays. They grew so hungry they began to worry they might eat each other!

One day, the boys held a meeting and lots were cast to choose who would dare go up and ask the master for more gruel after supper. The lot fell to Oliver.

Chapter Two

In Which
Oliver Asks
for More

That evening, the boys took their places
and the master served out the miserable
helpings of gruel from the great copper pot.
The ravenous youngsters quickly vanished
the gruel down their throats, then winked
at Oliver. Reckless with hunger, Oliver rose
from the table. He held out his bowl to the
master. "Please, sir, I want some more."

The well-fed master turned very pale.

Everyone was paralysed with fear.

"What!" whispered the master at last.

"Please, sir, I want some more."

The master hit Oliver over the head with
the ladle, grabbed him by the arms and
shrieked for the beadle. Mr Bumble marched
him straight off to the workhouse governors.

"That boy will come to be hung," the
governors cried in horror.

They ordered Mr Bumble to put a notice
on the workhouse gate, offering a five-pound

reward to any man or woman who would take Oliver Twist off the hands of the parish.

After that, Mr Bumble locked Oliver up in a cell. Every day, he came back and beat Oliver and Oliver cried bitter tears. Every night, the poor orphan shivered without a blanket, spread his little hands before his eyes to shut out the darkness, and tried to sleep. Many times during the long hours he would wake in fear and huddle closer to the wall, as if to find comfort from his loneliness in its cold, hard surface.

There he stayed for over a week.

Chapter Three
Oliver Forms an Unfavourable Notion of His New Master's Business

After that awful week had passed and no employer had been found for Oliver, the governors decided to send him as a cabin-boy on some trading vessel bound for foreign parts. Either Oliver would die of some terrible disease or the skipper would flog him to death. The board felt that either of these ends would be no less than Oliver deserved.

On his way to find a captain in need of a friendless boy, Mr Bumble met Mr Sowerberry, the local undertaker. He was a tall, gaunt man in a black threadbare suit, with darned stockings to match. Business was good for Mr Sowerberry and he was in need of a new boy apprentice – in fact, just such a boy as Oliver. So it was agreed that Mr Sowerberry should take Oliver to be his assistant. The governors told Oliver that he must either go with the coffin-maker or be sent to sea.

Poor Oliver wept until the tears sprang out from between his bony fingers.

"I am a very little boy, Mr Beadle, sir," said Oliver, "and it will be so lonely amongst the coffins."

Mr Bumble regarded Oliver in astonishment, then took his hand and marched him straight to the undertaker's shop.

Mrs Sowerberry, the undertaker's wife, was a mean woman. She took one look at Oliver and said in disgust, "Dear me! He's very small."

For supper she gave Oliver the scraps she'd kept by for the dog. Then she told him to make his bed among the coffins. Oliver felt as if he were lying in a graveyard, and

every moment expected some terrible form
to rise up and haunt him.

The next morning, Oliver met Mr
Sowerberry's assistant, Noah Claypole.
Noah was a large-headed, small-eyed bully,
who grew fond of kicking Oliver, pulling
his hair, twitching his ears and saying,
"I'll whop yer, work'us brat." He felt
himself very superior to Oliver.

Undertaking was a busy trade in those

days, as many people died of illness or
starvation. Oliver quickly got used to
measuring coffins, collecting bodies
and going to funerals. Oliver attended
more funerals than Noah on account
of his melancholy expression, which
Mr Sowerberry felt added dignity to the
funeral procession. Noah grew jealous
of Oliver and his taunts became more
frequent.

One day, Noah went too far and insulted
Oliver's dead mother. "She was a regular
right-down bad 'un!" he crowed.

Meek, tiny Oliver turned into a crimson
ball of fury. He attacked Noah with all the
force he could muster and knocked him to
the ground. Mrs Sowerberry rushed to

Noah's aid, and between them they
pommelled and scratched Oliver until
they were exhausted. When they were
done, they dragged poor Oliver into the coal
cellar and locked him up.

Noah ran to fetch Mr Bumble who
was convinced that Mrs Sowerberry had
been overfeeding Oliver. Both Mr Bumble
and Mr Sowerberry beat Oliver so that

even Mrs Sowerberry was satisfied, but
Oliver refused to cry.

Not until the night was dark, and Oliver
was again alone among the coffins, did he
fall to his knees and weep.

Early the next morning, before anyone
else was awake, Oliver packed a small
bundle, slipped out into the street and
set off for London.

Chapter Four
Oliver Walks to London and Encounters a Pleasant Old Gentleman

After seven days on the road, Oliver limped into Barnet, just outside London, and collapsed on a step.

"Hello, my covey, what's the row?"

Oliver looked up and saw a strange boy in huge clothes looking down at him. His name was Jack Dawkins, but he liked to be called "the Artful Dodger". Oliver told him of his

long journey and how very hungry and tired
he was. The Dodger helped Oliver up and
took him to a nearby public house, where he
treated Oliver to a long and hearty meal.

As Oliver ate, the Dodger talked: "Got
any lodgings? Money? Want some place to
sleep? I know a 'spectable old gentleman,"
he continued, "wot'll give you lodgings for
nothink, if I interduces you."

Tired as he was, this unexpected offer
of shelter was too tempting for Oliver
to resist.

The Dodger would not enter the city till
after dark, but as soon as night fell he led
Oliver through a maze of winding streets at
such a rapid pace that Oliver struggled to
keep up. Even in the dark, Oliver could

see and smell how filthy and wretched the streets were. He began to wonder whether he should run away. Then the Dodger drew him into a doorway.

They groped their way up the dark and broken stairs and into a back room.

A strange old man called Fagin was grilling sausages over a fire. He had matted red hair and wore a greasy flannel dressing gown.

Rows of silk handkerchiefs were strung

across the room, and around the table a gang of boys were drinking spirits and smoking long clay pipes.

"This is my friend Oliver Twist, Fagin," said the Dodger.

"We are very glad to see you, Oliver," said the old gentleman as he bowed deeply to Oliver. "Very."

Exhausted, Oliver ate a share of sausages, drank a glass of gin and hot water, and fell fast asleep.

Chapter Five
In Which Oliver Learns a New Game

It was late the next morning when Oliver awoke. The boys were gone and Fagin was gloating over a box of gold and jewels.

Suddenly, Fagin realized that Oliver was awake and watching him. He seized a bread knife and held it quivering in the air above Oliver's head.

"What have you seen?" he demanded. "Speak out, boy! Quick-quick for your life!"

Luckily for Oliver, at that very moment
there was a knock at the door, and in
walked Nancy. She was the girlfriend of
Fagin's partner, Bill Sikes. She was rather
red-cheeked, scruffy and hearty, and she
and Oliver took to each other at once.
Then the Dodger came back from work
with a boy called Charley Bates. They
brought more silk handkerchiefs with
them and a couple of fine leather wallets.
Fagin seemed very pleased and produced a

bottle of spirits, on account of the cold. The box of treasures was hidden, the knife returned to the bread and the conversation took on a merrier tone.

Fagin, the Dodger and Charley Bates proceeded to introduce Oliver to a very strange game indeed. Fagin hid things in his pockets and the Dodger and Charley had to try and take them out without his noticing. When it was his turn, Oliver had a go at removing a handkerchief from Fagin's pocket.

"Is it gone?" cried the old gentleman.

"Here it is, sir," said Oliver, showing it in his hand.

"You're a clever boy, my dear," said Fagin.

Oliver still didn't know what work the boys actually did, but as the days went by, he longed to go out with them. One morning, he was given the permission he so eagerly sought and the three boys went out together.

The Dodger and Charley walked so

slowly that Oliver feared they would be late for work. They came to a stop by a bookstall, and suddenly the Dodger plunged his hand into an old gentleman's pocket then ran off at speed.

All at once, Oliver realized that the boys were pickpockets. At the same moment, the old gentleman, whose name was Mr Brownlow, noticed his loss. Seeing only Oliver, he began to run after him.

"Stop thief, stop thief!" he shouted.

Soon everyone in the street had left their business and joined in the chase.

"Stop thief!"

"Stop thief!"

"Stop thief!"

Halted at last by a sideways blow, Oliver fell to the pavement, angry faces surrounding him. The old gentleman pushed his way through the crowd and looked down on Oliver with kind eyes.

"Poor fellow!" said Mr Brownlow. "He has hurt himself."

Ignoring Oliver's injuries, a police officer grabbed him by the collar and lugged him through the streets to the local magistrate.

Chapter Six
In Which Oliver Is Taken Better Care of than He Ever Was Before

Mr Fang, the magistrate, was a stern man. Oliver was trembling before him and very white. He murmured a feeble prayer for water and then fell to the ground in a faint.

"Take him away, officer," cried Mr Fang in disgust. "He is committed to three months' hard labour."

Just then the door flew open and the bookstall owner burst in.

"Stop, stop!" shouted the man. "I saw it all. Don't take him away!"

The bookstall owner told Mr Fang what had really happened, and Oliver was saved from prison but thrown out into the street.

A few moments later, Mr Brownlow found poor little Oliver lying on the pavement. His face was deadly white and his whole body shook from fever and shock.

"Poor boy, poor boy!" shouted Mr Brownlow. "Call a coach, there is no time to lose."

The old gentleman felt very sorry for Oliver.

He lifted him into his arms and took him back
to his home.

Oliver was ill for many weeks. He was
looked after by Mrs Bedwin, Mr Brownlow's
elderly housekeeper, who nursed him tenderly
and grew very fond of him. She called Oliver
her "pretty creetur". He had never known
such kindness or comfort.

As the weeks passed, Oliver gradually
grew stronger until he was well enough to
be carried downstairs to sit by the fire in

Mrs Bedwin's sitting room. Above the fireplace hung a portrait of a young woman, and when Mr Brownlow came to see Oliver, he was struck by how alike Oliver and the young woman were.

Oliver loved the portrait and said that the young lady was so pretty she made his heart beat faster!

When Oliver felt stronger, he grew anxious to repay the kindness of his new friends. So one day, when Mr Brownlow asked him to return some books and money for him, he rushed off at once.

As Oliver left, Mr Brownlow's friend Mr Grimwig was arriving for tea. Mr Grimwig was very fond of muffins, but not so fond of

trusting Oliver with the books and the money.

"If ever that boy returns to this house, sir," he said, "I'll eat my head."

Mr Brownlow was unruffled. He had absolute faith in Oliver and was sure he would be back in twenty minutes. "I'll answer to that boy's truth with my life!"

The two friends sat down to wait. Twenty minutes passed. An hour passed. At last it grew dark, but Oliver had not returned.

Chapter Seven
Oliver Is Claimed by Nancy and Locked Up

The morning that the Dodger and Charley Bates had come home without Oliver, Fagin and Bill Sikes had been furious. When he heard that Oliver had been arrested, released and then taken to Mr Brownlow's home, Fagin became even more agitated.

"He may say something which will get us into trouble," said Fagin.

So it was decided – against Nancy's wishes

– that she, Bill and Bill's dog, Bull's-eye, would keep watch on Mr Brownlow's house.

So as Oliver set out on his errand, Nancy and Bill grabbed him by the arms. Weak from his recent illness and terrified of the snarling dog, Oliver was powerless against them.

Back at Fagin's, Mr Brownlow's money and Oliver's new clothes were taken from him. Fagin hit Oliver over the shoulders with a club and would have continued, but Nancy stepped in and snatched the club away.

For over a week Oliver was kept prisoner,

alone and in the dark, until one night Nancy came to fetch him. She was white and agitated, and Oliver knew there was trouble ahead. Nancy told him that he was to go to the country on a job with Bill and that she wouldn't be able to protect him.

The next morning Oliver, Bill and Bull's-eye set out. They walked all day and half the night. At last, they reached a lonely house. Oliver realized Bill was going to burgle it, and he begged Bill to let him go.

"Get up, or I'll strew your brains upon the grass," hissed Bill.

Oliver tried to run away, but Bill grabbed him and lifted him up to a small window.

"Now listen, you young limb," hissed Bill. "Go along the little hall to the street-door;

unfasten it and let us in."

Bill put a lantern in Oliver's hand, pushed him through and trained his pistol on him.

Oliver had just decided to wake the family, instead of letting Bill in, when he heard a loud noise and felt a sharp pain in his arm. A servant had shot him!

Bill leaned in through the window, grabbed Oliver and dragged him out. Bill started to run, but when the servants gave chase he dumped Oliver's bleeding body into a ditch and made his escape, with Bull's-eye at his heels.

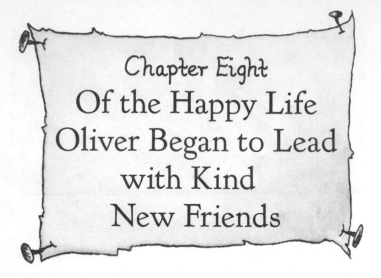

Chapter Eight
Of the Happy Life
Oliver Began to Lead
with Kind
New Friends

To Oliver's amazement, he woke up in a warm, comfortable bed. He had been ill for many weeks as a result of his wounded arm and exposure to wet and cold from the

journey. All that time he had been nursed by an old woman called Mrs Maylie and a younger one named Rose. Instead of calling a constable when they found Oliver, the kind ladies of the house that Bill Sikes had planned to rob had taken pity on him and called a doctor.

Mrs Maylie and Rose believed Oliver's story and took great care of him. Once his arm was healed, Rose promised to take him to London to see Mr Brownlow and explain things to him. Oliver was delighted.

"If they knew how happy I am, they would be pleased," he said.

"I am sure they would," smiled Rose.

Meanwhile, back in London, Bill had been ill since the failed burglary. Nancy had nursed him devotedly, but she had no money and she, Bill and Bull's-eye were thin and hungry. One night, Nancy went to borrow money from Fagin. While she was there, a man named Monks visited. Nancy listened in wonder at the words she overheard. The next evening, Nancy gave Bill a

sleeping draught and crept out. She went straight to the hotel that she had heard Monks mention. Rose Maylie and Oliver were staying there.

Nancy was terribly nervous.

"I have stolen away from those who would surely murder me," she said to Rose. She then told Rose what she had overheard – that Monks was Oliver's half-brother. Their father had left money to Oliver, on the condition that he did no wrong. Monks

was paying Fagin to recapture Oliver and turn him into a thief so that he wouldn't inherit! Nancy had risked her life to come to the hotel for Oliver and although Rose begged her to stay, Nancy refused because of her love for Bill.

"I am drawn back to him through every suffering and ill-usage," she sobbed as she turned to go.

"It wrings my heart to hear you," replied Rose, who was touched by Nancy's courage.

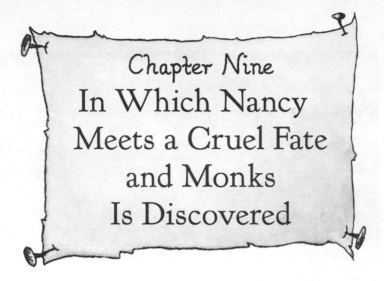

Chapter Nine
In Which Nancy Meets a Cruel Fate and Monks Is Discovered

The next day, Rose took Oliver to meet Mr Brownlow and Mrs Bedwin. How thrilled they both were at seeing Oliver again and having their faith in him restored.

"God be good to me!" cried Mrs Bedwin, embracing Oliver. "It is my innocent boy!"

"My dear old nurse!" cried Oliver.

Trusting Mr Brownlow at once, Rose confided Nancy's story to him.

Mr Brownlow was determined to track down Monks. So that night, he and Rose went to meet Nancy on London Bridge, where she had promised to be every Sunday at midnight. They followed Nancy down

some steps and into the shadows, where
she told them the name of a pub in which
Monks often drank and whispered a
description of him.

"A broad red mark, like a burn or scald!"
cried Mr Brownlow.

"How's this?" said Nancy. "You know
him!"

"I think I do," said the gentleman.

What none of them had guessed was

that the suspicious Fagin had sent Noah
Claypole, Oliver's old tormentor, to spy on
them and he had heard every word they
said. As Nancy hurried home, Noah was
hurrying back to Fagin.

When Noah told Fagin that Nancy had
betrayed Monks he fell into a foul rage.
He made Noah repeat his story to Bill,
but before the boy could finish, Bill rushed
away. He arrived home and pulled Nancy
from her bed.

"Spare my life for the love of heaven," she begged.

But Bill showed no mercy, and seizing a heavy club he struck poor Nancy dead.

* * *

It was thanks to Nancy, though, that Oliver was saved. Because of her bravery, Mr Brownlow knew how to find Monks. Doing so at once, he discovered that he was right – he did know the man. Monks' father, Edwin

Leeford, had been Mr Brownlow's oldest friend. Before his death, Leeford had been unhappily married to Monks's mother but had given Mr Brownlow a portrait of the woman he truly loved: Agnes Fleming.

It was this picture that had so startled Mr Brownlow with its likeness to Oliver!

Chapter Ten
And Last

After Nancy's death, Fagin was arrested
and the boys and Bill went into hiding in
a ruined house. One night, a suspicious
crowd gathered outside it.

"In the King's name, break down the
door!" roared the throng.

"I'll cheat you yet!" cried Bill.

Climbing out onto the parapet to escape,
Bill tied a rope around the chimney

intending to jump to the ground. As
he slipped the rope around himself, he
imagined he saw Nancy's dying face, lost
his footing and slid off the roof. The noose
tightened around his neck and he swung
lifeless. The chimney shook and Bull's-eye
let out a dismal howl. He tried to spring

onto the dead man's shoulders, but
missed his aim, crashed to the ground
and died.

And now this story is almost ended.
Oliver was to see Fagin once more –
in prison. He and Mr Brownlow went
to ask him about some of Monks's papers.

"It's not a sight for children, sir,"
warned the jailer.

Fagin had lost his wits. Meek and
enraged by turns, he took Oliver by
the shoulders and tried to escape with
him. The guard pulled him back, but
his shrieks followed Oliver and Mr
Brownlow out of the prison and past

the gallows where he was to be hanged
the very next morning.

The Dodger and Noah Claypole
were shocked by Fagin's death and
appalled by Bill's crime against Nancy.
They both decided that an honest life
might be best. It was a struggle, but in
the end they succeeded!

Monks did not fare so well. He took a share of Oliver's inheritance and left for the New World, where he quickly squandered the money, returned to a life of crime and died in jail.

As for young Oliver, Mr Brownlow adopted him and moved with Mrs Bedwin to the country, close to Rose and Mrs Maylie.

A stone was set near the altar of the local church, in memory of Agnes Fleming.

Whenever he can, Mr Grimwig visits on Sundays to fish and eat muffins. Mr Brownlow often reminds him of how wrong he was to say Oliver would not come back. And often, Mr Grimwig promises to eat his head. "Well, I'll eat my head!"

But he never has!

THE END

Charles Dickens

Charles Dickens was a respected novelist who lived in Victorian England. He went to various schools until he started work aged fifteen – although he spent an unhappy period labouring in a factory when he was twelve. He wrote fourteen novels and many other shorter stories, becoming the most famous writer of the time. He died in 1870.

What the Dickens!

Marcia Williams

Marcia Williams' mother was a novelist and her father a playwright, so it's not surprising that Marcia ended up an author herself. Her distinctive comic-strip style goes back to her schooldays in Sussex and the illustrated letters she sent home to her parents overseas.

Although she never trained formally as an artist, she found that motherhood, and the time she spent later as a nursery school teacher, inspired her to start writing and illustrating children's books.

Marcia's books bring to life some of the world's all-time favourite stories and some colourful historical characters. Her hilarious retellings and clever observations will have children laughing out loud and coming back for more!

Books in this series

ISBN 978-1-4063-5692-2

ISBN 978-1-4063-5695-3

ISBN 978-1-4063-5693-9

ISBN 978-1-4063-5694-6

Available from all good booksellers

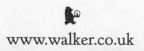